MEL BAY PRESENTS

SONGS OF LATIN AMERICA

By Jerry Silverman

CONTENTS

El Carretero
The Cartman

The *chacarera* is a country dance that originated in the northern provinces of Argentina, during the latter part of the 19th century. Its rural roots are evident from its name, which derives from *chacra*, the word for farm.

Argentina

Chacarera

Ca - rre - te - ro, ca - rre - te - ro, ca - rre - te - ro de jun -
O, you cart-man, o, you cart - man, o, you cart-man, roll - ing

cal, el o - to - ño trai - cio - ne - ro, ha se -
free, It's the treach-'rous au - tumn wea - ther that has

ca - do mi ro - sal. Ca - rre - te - ro, ca - rre -
killed my lit - tle tree. O, you cart - man, o, you

te - ro e - se ro - sal es mi a - mor. El o - to - ño trai - cio - ne - ro tu ca -
cart - man, that rose-bush it is my love. O, you treach-rous au - tumn wea-ther, O, you

ri - ño en-ga - ña - dor. (hablado) Así cantó la charerita. Cuando? Ha-ce un ra -
dear un - faith - ful one. (spoken) So sang the farm-er girl. When? A mo - ment

ti - to que la cha-ca - re - ra por la ca - rre - te - ra can-tan-do pa -
has just passed by since the farm-er girl did sing her song while walk-ing down the

só, en - ton - an-do es - ta cha-caya-le - ra con voz pla-ñi -
road, And she sang this plain-tive lit - tle mel - o - dy which could be

4

de - ra que tris - te se o - yó. Ha ce un ra - ti - to que la cha - ca
heard so sad - ly far and near. A mo - ment has just passed by since the

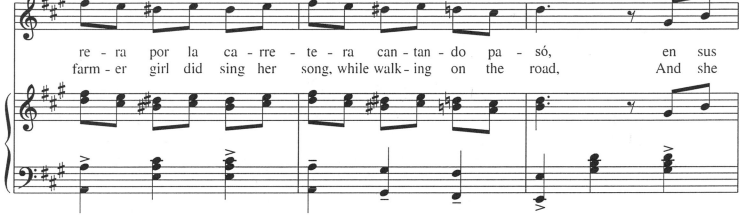

re - ra por la ca - rre - te - ra can - tan - do pa - só, en sus
farm - er girl did sing her song, while walk - ing on the road, And she

ver - sos di - cien - do do - lor - es de his - tor - ia en a - mo - res que tris - te se o - yó.
sang this plain - tive lit - tle mel - o - dy, which could be heard so sad - ly far and near.

Carretero, carretero,
te llevastes mi querer.
carretero, carretero,
para nunca más volver,
que no has de volver si es cierto,
carretero como hay ser,
donde una esperanza ha muerto,
otra hay volver a nacer.
Así cantaba la chacarerita
Cuando?   *Chorus*

O, you cartman, o you cartman,
You have carried off my heart.
O, you cartman, o, you cartman,
Nevermore I'll see your cart.
If it's sure that you won't come back,
Then I guess it has to be,
But where on fond hope lies dying,
Then another one I'll see.
So sang the farmer-girl.
When?   *Chorus*

Vidalita
My Little Life

This lively, bouncing dance is reminiscent of the Polish mazurka. Much of Argentinean culture has always had a decidedly European caste.

Argentina   Vidala

Des - de que te fuis - te,   mi a-man - te bien,
Since you've gone a - way,   my be - lov - ed one,

No hay un dul - ce dí - a.   Pá - li - das las ho - ras pa-sar se ven,
There's not been a sweet   day.   And the pal - lid hours, slow - ly they pass by,

Po - bre suer - te mí - a.   Al - ma de mi al -
O, my fate is   so   sad.   Dear soul of my soul,

ma, la blan - ca flor, Que al par - tir me dis - te.   Se do - bló a-ba - ti -
When you went a - way, You gave me a white flower.   It's dropped to the ground,

6

da, per-dió el co-lor, Va mu-rien do-tris - te. Pá - li-das las ho-
Fad - ed quite a - way, Sad - ly it is dy - ing. And the pal - lid hours,

ras pa-sar se ven, Po-bre suer-te mí - a. a._____
slow-ly they pass by, O, my fate is so sad. sad._____

Tanta es la tristeza de mi pesar, tan amargo el llanto,
Que con él regarla fuera a matar la flor de mi encanto.
Vuelve, oh vida, y trae para la flor, agua de la fuente,
A su blando riego, flor del amor, te alzarás sonriente,
Pálidas las horas pasar se ven, pobre suerte mía.

So great is the sorrow, I am weighed down and I weep bitter tears.
As they showered down, their droplets did kill my enchanted white flower
Come back, o my life, and bring for the flower water from the fountain.
By this gentle rain, flower of my heart, you shall rise up smiling.
And the pallid hours, slowly they pass by - o, my fate is so sad.

Te Lo Contaré
I'll Tell You All About It

The pentatonic structure of this typical *huaino* clearly points to its Indian origins.

Bolivia   Huaino

Te lo con - ta - ré a tí pu -
I'll tell you all a - bout it,

es, te lo____ bai - la - ré.   A quien más
Then I'll dance it just for you.   Whom do you

quie - ras a - sí, pues te la____ tra - e - ré.
love the fond - est, I will steal____ her a - way.

Calzados bayos para tí,	Think you're so smart in your brown shoes,
El taco restares,	You'll be down at the heel.
De lejos que vean pues	From far off all your friends can see
Las amistades.	Just the way you do feel.

Calla, No Llores
Hush, Don't Cry

Yaravi is a word in the Guarani Indian language. It is a dance form.

Bolivia   Yaravi

E - res pa - ra mí más dul - ce que el re - cuer - do de la in -
To me you are so much sweet - er than the re - mem - brance of

fan - cia, Ca - lla, no llo - res co - ra - zón.
child-hood, O hush, and don't you cry, my heart.

En tu a-lien - to hay más fra - gan - cia que per - fu - me en ca - da flor. Ca -
And in your breath there's more fra - grance than the per - fume of each flow'r. O

10

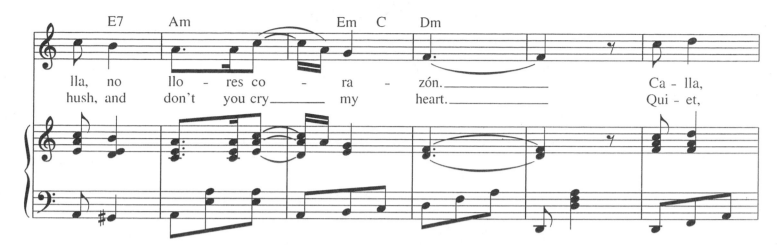

lla, no llo - res co - ra - zón. _____ Ca - lla,
hush, and don't you cry _____ my heart. _____ Qui - et,

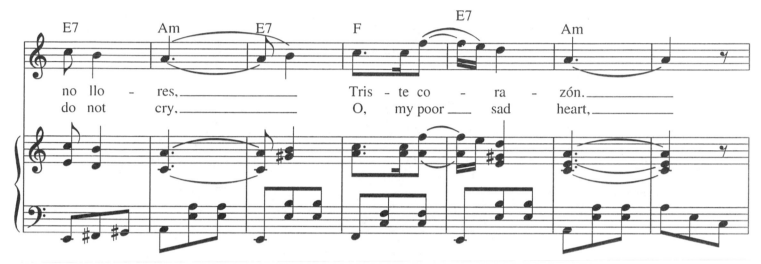

no llo - res, _____ Tris - te co - ra - zón. _____
do not cry, _____ O, my poor ___ sad heart, _____

Con el llan - to no se a - pa - ga el ar - dor de u - na pa - sión. Ca -
For cry - ing nev - er can sti - fle fi - e - ry pas - sion - ate flames, O

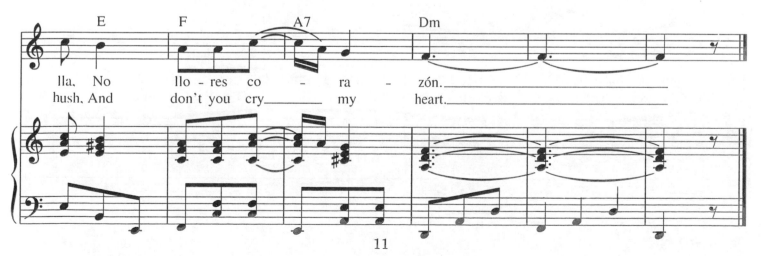

lla, No llo - res co - ra - zón. _____
hush, And don't you cry _____ my heart. _____

Tutú Marambá

If the baby doesn't fall asleep, the evil spirit *Tutú Marambá* will come and eat it. Not exactly a soothing bedtime
story, but think of all the scary Mother Goose and Grimm fairy tales you heard as a child. To make matters even worse,
the spider, *Aranha Tatanha* ("aranya tatanya") is also keeping his eye on things in company with *Tatú*, the armadillo.

Brazil

Tu - tú Ma-ram-bá, não ve - nhas mais cá, que o pai do-me-ni - no te
Tu - tú Ma-ram-bá if you come this way, The ba - by's fa - ther will

man - da ma-tá. Tu - tú Ma-ram-bá não ve - nhas mais cá, que o
chase you a-way; Tu - tú Ma-ram-bá, if you come this way. The

pai do-me-ni - no te man - da ma - tá! Dor-m en-gra - ça - di - nho, Pe - que-
ba - by's fa - ther will chase you a - way! Go to sleep my ba - by, Love-ly

Fine

ni - no da ma-mãe, Qu'e-le é bo - ni - ti - nho, e fi - lhi-no da ma-mãe! A -
lit - tle pet of mine, Beau-ti - ful and hap-py be, O lit - tle child of mine! A -

12

ra - nha Ta-ta - nha, A - ra - nha Ta-ti - nha, Ta-tú an - dar - ra-nhan - do a
ra - nha Ta-ta - nha, A - ra - nha Ta-ti - nha, Ta-tú your house is scratch - ing to

tu - a ca - si - nha, A - ra - nha Ta-ta - nha, A - ra - nha Ta-ti - nha, Ta-
see if you are sleep - ing, A - ra - nha Ta-ta - nha, A - ra - nha Ta-ti - nha, Ta-

tú é que ar-ra - nha, A tu - a ca - si - nha. Dor-m'en gra - ça - di - nho, pe - que-
tú will be glad when he finds you are sleep - ing. Go to sleep, my ba - by, love -ly

ni - no da ma - mãe; Qu'e-le é bo - ni - ti - nho, E fi - lhi - no da ma - mãe! Tu -
lit - tle pet of mine, Beau - ti - ful and hap - py be, O lit - tle child of mine! Tu -

D. C. al Fine

Morena, Morena

Morena is the dark-complexioned woman, whose beauty runs like a thread through many Latin American songs.
The word itself derives from "moor" (as in "Othello, the Moor of Venice").

Brazil

man - tes.   Mo-re-na,   Mo-re - na,   Mo-re-na, Mo-
dia - monds.   Mo-re-na,   Mo-re - na,   Mo-re-na, Mo-

re - na,   Mo-re-na,   Mo-re - na,   Tem pe-na   de
re - na,   Mo-re-na,   Mo-re - na,   Take pi-ty on

mim.   Mo-re-na, Mo-re - na,   Mo-re-na, Mo-re - na,
me.   Mo-re-na, Mo-re - na,   Mo-re-na, Mo-re - na,

Mo-re-na, Mo-re - na,   Tem pe-na de mim.
Mo-re-na, Mo-re - na,   Take pi-ty on me.

15

Mi Caballo Blanco
My White Horse

Chile

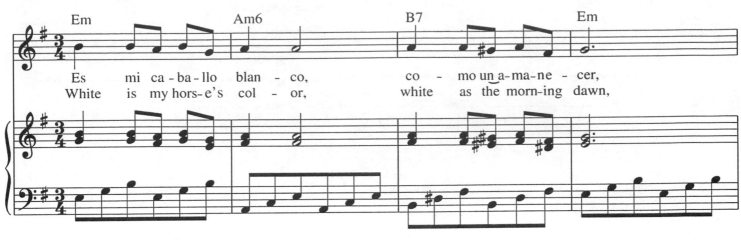

Es mi ca-ba-llo blan-co, co-mo un a-ma-ne-cer,
White is my hors-e's col-or, white as the morn-ing dawn,

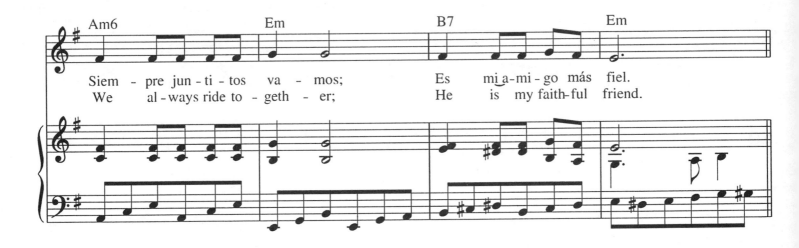

Siem-pre jun-ti-tos va-mos; Es mi a-mi-go más fiel.
We al-ways ride to-geth-er; He is my faith-ful friend.

Chorus

Mi ca-ba-llo, Mi ca-ba-llo, Gal-o-pan-do va.
My faith-ful horse, My faith-ful horse, Gal-lo-ping a-long.

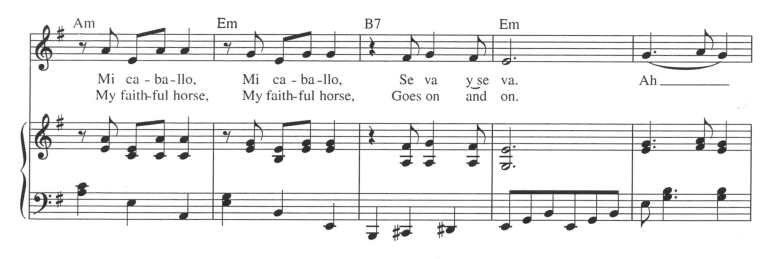

Mi ca - ba -llo,   Mi ca - ba -llo,   Se va   y se va.   Ah _____

My faith-ful horse,   My faith-ful horse,   Goes on   and on.

Ah _____   Ah _____   Ah   Ah.

En alas de una dicha
Mi caballo corrió,
Y en brazos de una pena
También él me llevó.   *Chorus*

Hasta que a Dios le pido
Que lo tenga muy bien,
Si a su lado me llama,
En mi blanquito iré.   *Chorus*

Riding on wings of gladness,
My white horse carried me.
And in the arms of sadness,
Together we shall be.   *Chorus*

I ask the Lord to keep him,
Safe - and to be his guide.
And when the Lord shall call me,
On Whitey I shall ride.   *Chorus*

Ámame Mucho
Love Me As Much

(As I Love You)

A typical *cueca* presents contrasting metrical sections: a heavily accented introduction (and interlude) in "three," and the main body of the song in "six."

Chile   Cueca

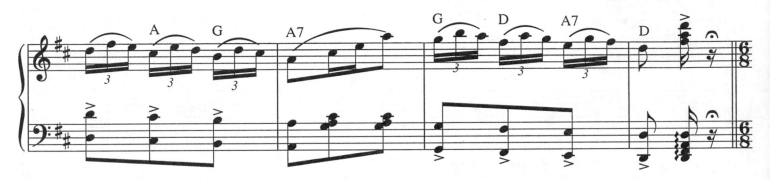

A - llá en la no - che ca - lla - da pa - ra que se oi - ga me - jor___
Far   off in the qui - et   night so   it can be   heard   much bet - ter___

___   Á - ma - me   mu - cho que a - sí a - mo   yo._____   A
___   Love me as   much as I do love   you._____   Far

yo._____ Can -ta el rui - se - ñõr sus pe - nas, Ay si!_____ Ay
you._____ The night-in-gale sings his sor - rows, - O yes!_____ O

no!_____ Can -ta el rui - se - ñor sus pe - nas___ con me - lan - có - li - ca
no!_____ The night-in-gale sings his sor - rows___ with a mel - an - cho -ly

voz,_____ Á - ma - me mu - cho que a - sí a - mo yo._____
voice,_____ Love me as much as I do love you._____

El Zancudo
The Mosquito

Colombia

E - ché mis per - ros al mon - te, El u - no la - tió muy
I sent my dogs to the moun - tain, And there was a loud com -

du - ro. El a - mo se fué a - so - mar, Y er' un in - fe - liz zan -
motion. When I ran up and looked a - round, A mo - squi - to was set in

cu - do. Cla - vé mi ro - dill - a en tier - ra, Y a - pun - té bien a - pun -
mo - tion. I dug my heel in the ground then, And care - ful - ly aimed my

ta - o, Y fue tan grand' el ba - la - zo Que que - dó pa - ta - rri - ba - o.
ri - fle. The bul - let, it hit him so hard, That you know it was no tri - fle.

Pa matar ese animal
Se tendió l'infantería
Con quince ametralladoras
Y un cañón d'infantería.
    La carne d'este animal
    La mandaron pa Marmato
    Pesaba dos mil arrobas,
    Catorce libros y cuarto.

El sebo d'este animal
Lo mandaron p'al Tabor.
Eso hace quinientos años,
Y todavía hay jabón.
    Del cuero d'ese animal
    Salieron dos mil paraguas,
    Y un pedazo que sobró
    Se lu'hizo una vieja en naguas.

In order to kill this monster,
The army, it had to be called up,
With fifteen machine guns blazing -
A cannon was also rolled up.
    The flesh of this great mosquito
    Was sent off to feed Marmato.
    Five thousand pounds it did weigh,
    Plus forty more pounds and a quarter.

The fat of this great mosquito
Was sent over to Tabor.
That was five hundred years ago -
Of soap, they still need no more.
    The hide yielded up two thousand
    Umbrellas for rainy weather.
    And from the small piece left over,
    A fine skirt was stitched together.

Van Cantando Por La Sierra
O'er The Mountain They Go Singing

Colombia

Van can -tan -do por la sie -rra con hon - da me-lan-co-
O'er the moun - tain they go sing - ing with sad - ness and mel-an-

lí -a,_____ U -nos can -tos de mi tie -rra,_____
cho -ly,_____ And they sing songs of my coun -try,_____

___ Cuan -do va mu -rien-do el dí - a. Ti -ñe el a -zul ho -ri -
___ As the day -light turns to eve - ning. And the blue ho -ri -zon's

zon -te u -na lu -mi -no -sa fran -ja,_____ Que da
tint -ed by a fringe of fad -ing sun -light,_____ That gives

a	los lla-nos y al mon-te	sua-ve co-lor de na-ran-ja,	
to	the plains and the moun-tain	a glow-ing au-ra of or-ange,	

Sua-ve co-lor de na-ran-ja.

A glow-ing au-ra of or-ange.

Canta el ave enamorada
En el follaje sombrío,
Y murmura en la enramada
Su extraño lenguaje al río.

Se escucha el suave concento
De hojarascas y bejucos,
Mientras que se lleva el viento
El eco de mis bambucos.

And the lovesick bird is singing,
As the somber leaves do quiver;
How it murmurs in the branches,
In its language, by the river.

Gentle sounds are heard all mingled,
Of the dried leaves and lianas,
While the rising wind does carry
The echo of my *bambucos.* *

* bambuco, a dance

¡Ay! Tituy

Costa Rica

¡Ay! ti - tuy,_____ ¡Ay! ti - tuy,_____ ¡Ay! ti - tuy qui - ni - nuy, qui - ni -

nuy._____ ¡Ay! ti - tuy,_____ ¡Ay! ti - tuy,_____ ¡Ay! ti -

tuy, qui - ni nuy, qui - ni - nuy._____ ¡Ay! ti - tuy,_____ La
The

pie - dra que mu - cho rue - da_____ no sir - ve pa - ra ci -
stone that keeps on a - roll - ing,_____ Won't make a sol - id foun -

mien-to _____ co-mo el hom - bre _____ sin ver - güen - za _____ que no
da - tion, _____ Like the man who _____ loves the la - dies, But _____ who shuns

tra - ta de ca - sa - mien - to. _____ La mien - to. _____ ¡Ay! ti -
mar - riag - e's com - pli - ca - tions. _____ The ca - tions. _____

to 𝄋
Chorus

Me dices que no me quieres,
Porque no te he dado nada.
Acordate del centavo
Que te dí el año pasado. *Chorus*

Me dices que no me quieres,
Porque yo te dí mal pago.
Volveme a querer de nuevo,
Porque un clavo saca otro clavo. *Chorus*

You say that you do not love me,
And that I gave you nothing.
Just remember that *centavo*
That I gave to you just last spring. *Chorus*

You say that you do not love me,
Because I paid you poorly.
Come back once more and love me -
One nail drives another surely. *Chorus*

El Toro Pinto
The Spotted Bull

Costa Rica

E - chá - me e se - to ro - pin - to, Hi - jo de la va - ca mo - ra, Pa -
Re - lease me that spot - ted bull now, The son of the mot - tled old cow, My

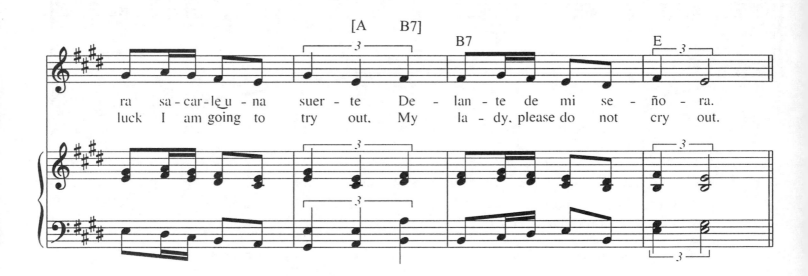

ra sa - car le u - na suer - te De - lan - te de mi se - ño - ra.
luck I am going to try out, My la - dy, please do not cry out.

Chorus

Que te co - ge el to - ro, Si - mo - na, Que te co - ge el to - ro, Mar - ce - la!
O! the bull will get you, Si - mo - na, O, The bull will get you, Mar - ce - la!

26

Si ese toro me matare,
No me entierren en sagrado.
Entiérrenme en campo afuera,
Donde me pise el ganado. *Chorus*

No murió de calentura,
Ni de dolor al costado;
Murió de una cornada
Que le dió el toro pintado. *Chorus*

Allá en aquél rincón
Pintado de colorado,
Allí están las cinco letras
Donde murió el desdichado. *Chorus*

And if this brave bull does kill me,
Don't bury me in the churchyard,
Just lay my bones on the prairie,
Where cattle will trample on me. *Chorus*

He didn't die of a fever,
Nor of some pain in his body,
But rather a vicious goring;
The bull left him lying bloody. *Chorus*

And in some forgotten corner,
Now reddened by his blood flowing,
There marked by a plain inscription,
Died the unlucky bullfighter. *Chorus*

Bañado El Rostro
Bathed Was Her Fair Face

The infectious rhythm of the *habanera* may be heard as the accompaniment to songs and dances all over Latin America. Perhaps the most famous *habanera* was composed by a Frenchman (Bizet) to be sung by a Spanish gypsy (Carmen).

Cuba   Habanera

Ba - ña-do el / Bathed was her
ros - tro, En luz di-vi - na, Cán-di-da y pu - ra,
fair face in light ce-les - tial, In-no-cent, pure, a
be-lla y a - sí, Co-mo es-as co - sas que son de
beau-ty to see. As with these things that come down from
cie - lo u-na ma-ña - na la co-no-cí. E-ra tan
heav - en one ear-ly morn-ing she came to me. It was so

pu - ra _____ la ne - gra no - che _____ que vi - ne al mun - do _____
dark then, _____ When night de - scend - ed _____ up - on this poor earth, _____

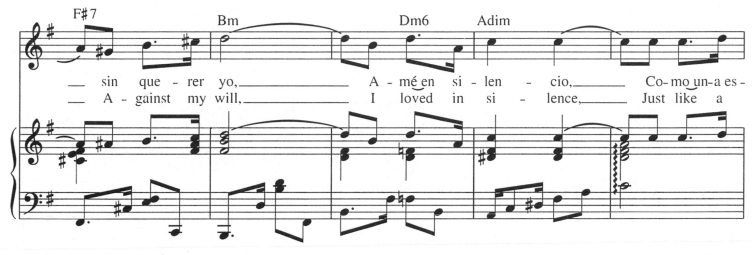

__ sin que - rer yo, _____ A - mé en si - len - cio, _____ Co - mo un - a es -
__ A - gainst my will, _____ I loved in si - lence, _____ Just like a

cla - va, _____ Se pu - so en - fer - mo _____ mi co - ra - zón, _____
poor slave, _____ And though my heart breaks, _____ I love her still, _____

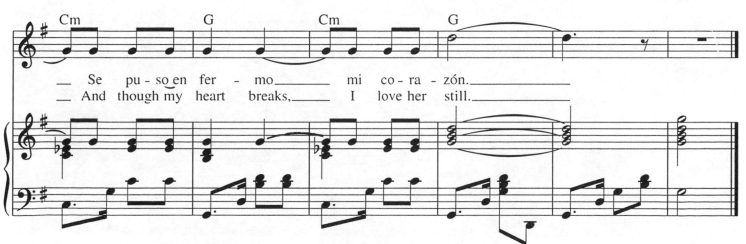

__ Se pu - so en - fer - mo _____ mi co - ra - zón.
__ And though my heart breaks, _____ I love her still. _____

30

La Tarde
The Evening

Although the *bolero* is of Spanish origin, and here transported to Cuba, as with the "Bizet-*habanera* connection," it remained for another French composer, Maurice Ravel, to write the *bolero* that has come to symbolize this dance all over the world.

Cuba

Bolero

Em
La luz que en tus ojos arde, Si
The light in your bright eyes burning, Like
G7
C
los abres amanece, Cuan-
dawn shines out when they're open, But
B7
C
do los cierras parece que
when you close them, it seems like the

D7   D♯dim Em

va _____ mu - rien - do la tar - de, _____ cuan -
eve - ning light __ is fast fad - ing, _____ But

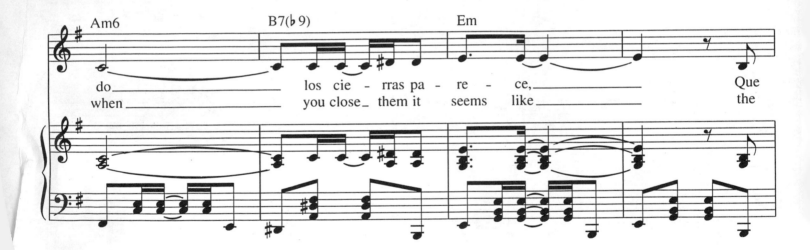

Am6   B7(♭9)   Em

do _____ los cie - rras pa - re - ce, _____ Que
when _____ you close __ them it seems like _____ the

B7   Em

va   mu - rien - do la tar - de, _____
eve - ning light is fast fad - ing. _____

Las pe - nas que a mí me ma - tan,__
The sor - rows that_ do as - sail me,__

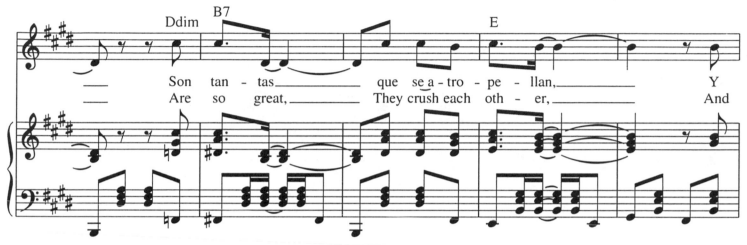

Son tan - tas__ que se a-tro-pe - llan,__ Y
Are so great,__ They crush each oth - er,__ And

co - mo__ de ma-tar me tra - tan,_ se a-gol-pan u - nas a
since they__ are try-ing to kill me,_ They fight a-mong_ them-selves;

o - tras, y por e - so no me ma - tan.__
And that is__ the rea - son they don't kill me.__

Tomá Juyó
Tomás Ran Away

This is the earliest known *merengue*, the dance that has become the "national dance" of the Dominican Republic. It dates from the Battle of Talanquera, in 1844, between opposing Dominican and Haitian soldiers. Under Haitian attack, a certain Tomás Torres abandoned his station, fleeing with the Dominican flag. Eventually the Dominican troops counterattacked and won the day. Soon after the battle, Dominican soldiers began singing and dancing this song, ridiculing the cowardly behavior of the runaway Torres.

As with most new forms of popular music (think of ragtime, jazz and rock 'n' roll in our own country), the Dominican musical "establishment" started out by being virulently anti-*merengue*. Poems were written in outrage with lines like: *el torpe merengue aborrecible* (the crude and despicable *merengue*), and *hijo digno del diablo y de una furia...tú villano, que insultas al pudor* (true son of the devil and a fury...you villain, who insults chastity). But the *merengue* (like ragtime, etc.) hung on and had the last laugh.

Dominican Republic   Merengue

To - má___ ju - yó con la___ ban - de - ra,___
To - más,___ He ran a - way in ter - ror,___

To - má___ ju - yó de Ta - lan___ que - ra;___
To - más,___ He fled from Ta - lan - que - ra;___

Si jue - ra yo, Yo no___ ju - ye - ra,___
If it___ were I, I'd still___ be there - a;___

34

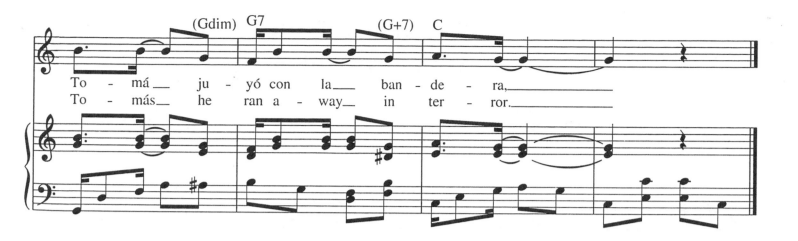

To - má ___ ju - yó con la ___ ban - de - ra, _____
To - más ___ he ran a - way ___ in ter - ror. _____

Duérmete, Mi Niño
Sleep, My Child

This tender lullaby originated in Spain, and is sung in a number of other Latin American countries including the Dominican Republic.

Dominican Republic

Duér - me-te, mi ni - ño, Duér - me-te mi a- mor,_____
Sleep, my lit - tle ba - by, Sleep, my lit - tle dove,_____

Duer - me dul - ce en-can - to de mi co - ra - zón._____
Sleep, you sweet en - chant - ment of your moth - er's love.

Ay, mi Palomita,	O my little pigeon,
la que yo adoré.	One that I adored,
que nació allá	Born so far away.
y voló se fué.	Will return no more.
Ella no comía	It would never eat food,
ni trigo ni arroz,	Neither rice nor wheat;
y se mantenía	All it ever needed,
sólo con amor. *Repeat first verse*	Was my love so sweet.

36

Kurikinga

A *kurikinga* is a bird. In this context it is applied to a lively, vivacious woman.

Ecuador

Ku - ri - kin - ga, ma - pa - ña - wi, Ku - ri - kin - ga, ma - pa - ña - wi, Da la me - dia
Ku - ri - kin - ga, two-faced wo - man, Ku - ri - kin - ga, two-faced wo - man. Swing half-way a -

vuel - ta, Ku - ri - kin - ga, Da la vuel - ta en - te - ra, Ku - ri - kin - ga, Me - nea que me - ne - a, Ku - ri-
round now, Ku - ri - kin - ga, Swing a - round and 'round now, Ku - ri - kin - ga, shake it, ba - by, shake it, Ku - ri-

kin - ga, Be - be la co - pi - ta, Ku - ri - kin - ga, Has - ta que te can - ses, Ku - ri - kin - ga. Ku - ri-
kin - ga, Drink a lit - tle whis - ky, Ku - ri - kin - ga, It will make you fris - ky, Ku - ri - kin - ga. Ku - ri-

kin - ga, ma - pa - ña - wi, Ku - ri - kin - ga, ma - pa - ña - wi, Da la me - dia vuel - ta, Ku - ri - kin - ga.
kin - ga, Two - faced wo - man, Ku - ri - kin - ga, two - faced wo - man, Swing half-way a - round now, Ku - ri - kin - ga.

Separación
Separation

The Christianized Indians of the Andes adopted many saints as their own. San Juan (St. John) is, perhaps, their favorite. A *sanjuanito* is dance performed before the many shrines erected in that saint's honor.

Ecuador

Sanjuanito

38

To - rren - te de lá - gri - mas a mí me cos - tó, To -
A tor - rent of bit - ter, tears I had __ to shed, A

rren - te de lá - gri - mas a mí me cos - tó, Sa - lir de mi tie - rra don -
tor - rent of bit - ter fears I had __ to shed, To part from the land where I

de na - cí yo, Sa - lir de mi tie - rra don - de na - cí yo.
was born and bred, To part from the land where I was born and bred.

Fine

Tris-te, muy tris - te la
Sad sep - a - ra - tion, It's

se - par-a - ción,   Tris - te, Muy tris - te la se - par-a - ción   por que en au - sen - cia se
hard to de -part,   Sad sep-a - ra - tion, It's hard to de -part,   Leav - ing the land that is

guar - da pa - sión,   Por que en au - sen - cia se guar - da pa - sión.
dear to my heart,   Leav - ing the land that is dear to my heart.

To -
A

40

Vamos A La Mar
Let's Go To The Sea

Guatemala

Vamos a la mar, tum tum,
A comer pescado, tum tum,
Frito y asado, tum tum,
En sartén de palo, tum tum.

Let's go to the sea, tum tum,
Any way you do it, tum tum,
Eat them fried or roasted, tum tum,
Or you barbecue it, tum tum.

Nací En La Cumbre
I Was Born On The Mountain

Guatemala

Na - cí en la cum - bre de u - na mon - ta - ña, Li - bran-do el
Up - on a moun - tain is where I was___ born, The sun was

ra - yo de - vas - ta - dor; Cre-cí en el fon - do de u - na ca -
shin - ing down from the sky; And in a ca - bin is where I

ba - ña, Y hoy que soy hom - bre, mue - ro de a - mor.
grew up, Now I'm a grown man, From love I die.

Unos bandidos me alimentaron,	Well, I was fed by a band of outlaws,
A la cuitada que me dió el ser;	And the poor woman who gave me birth,
Hijo del Trueno me apellidaron,	They all did call me the son of Thunder,
Y en noche obscura vine a nacer.	Since that dark night - my first on earth.
Si tú no sales a tu ventana,	If you don't come to your bedroom window,
Perla de Oriente, nítida flor,	Pearl of the Orient, my pretty flower,
Cabe tus muros verás mañana	Against your wall you will see tomorrow,
Rota mi lira, muerto al cantor.	The broken lyre of my final hour.

Sherman Collection, National Park Service

Les Emigrés
The Emigrants

Haitian *emigrés* coming to New York in the early 1930s faced the usual discrimination accorded most black immigrants. Their unfortunate situation was exacerbated by the Depression. Nevertheless, a ray of hope still shines through this song.

Haiti

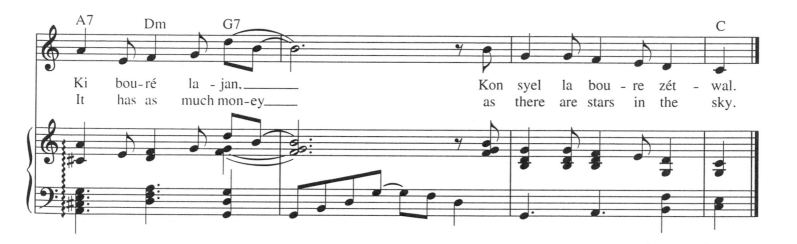

Ki bou-ré la - jan,_____ Kon syel la bou-re zét - wal.

It has as much mon-ey_____ as there are stars in the sky.

Nou Yòk se yon vil
Ki pa kab konté
Diferan peplad
Ki groupé ladan'l.
Kanta bél medam,
Ranpli detiket,
Yo sanble ti zanj
Ki soti nan syel.
Lóganizasyon
Vi Nou Yòk la
Fe tout moun maché
Na dwa chemen.
An deyò de sa,
Nou jwenn tout bagay,
Mwen pa kwe Leròp
Kapab fé pou nou. *Chorus*

Si w rivé Nou Yòk,
Lo w fin pale anglé,
Ou pa fè lanjan,
S'on krim w ap peyé.
Kar nenpòt nasyon
Ki rantre Nou Yòk,
Apre kèk ané,
Li tounen Kresus.
Avan kek ané,
Li gentan maryé.
La pe banboché
Avek madanm li.
Li vin gen oto,
Li vin gen bilding.
Si nou kwè'm manti,
Al mande Jwif yo.

Chorus 2:
Devan yon dpisè parèy,
Yo fe yo Ameriken,
Pou yo siveyé
Leurs propres intérêts
Se pa yon dezoné,
Se pa yon lacheté,
Se to simpman
Yon devwa yo ranpli.

Chorus 3:
Nou zòt pitit Etiopi,
Lè nou rivé bo la,
Sa réd pou nou jwenn yon
   rout,
Nou tonbé an derout.
Nou mèt tann nwit kon jou,
Chemen baré pou nou.
Se yon dezespwa
Pou nom ki gen po nwa.

New York is a town
Which just cannot count
The different groups
Of people here found.
Its women are beauties,
And have great charm.
They are just like angels
Down from the skies.
The way life is run
Right here in New York,
Makes every man
Just stick to his work.
And what's even more,
There's so much around,
I don't think Europe
Could do more for us. *Chorus*

So when you get here,
And English you learn,
If you don't do well,
It would be a crime.
For any nation
That comes to New York,
After a few years
Becomes like Croesus.
And then pretty soon
They all get married,
Enjoy a good life
With their darling wife.
Then they buy a car,
Then buy a building.
If you think I'm lying,
Go ask the Jews.

Chorus 2:
Because of such good luck,
They become citizens,
In order to protect
Their proper interests.
It's not a dishonor,
It is not cowardice.
It's simply a matter
Of doing what must be done.

Chorus 3:
But we Ethiopian sons,
When we come to these shores,
It's hard to find the path,
And so we often fail.
Though we wait nights and days,
The road is blocked for us.
A hopeless condition
For him who's born with black
   skin.

Feuille - o
Leaves - o

The distraught mother calls out to the spirit of the leaves, *feuille-o* ("feyo") to save the life of her sick child.
The *gan-gan* is the witch doctor or medicine man.

Haiti

Feuille - o,___ sau - vez la vie moin,___ nan mi - ser moin ye -
Leaves - o,___ won't you save my life,___ won't you end my suf -

o.
f'ring?

o.
f'ring?

Pi - tit moin ma - lad,___ M' cou - ri
O, my child is sick___ I'll run to

caille gan-gan,___ Si - mi - lo._____
the *gan gan,*___ Hear my cry._____
     (2nd time) Si li
     And a

Pi - tit bon gan-gan,___ La sau-vez
O, my good *gan gan*___ will save my

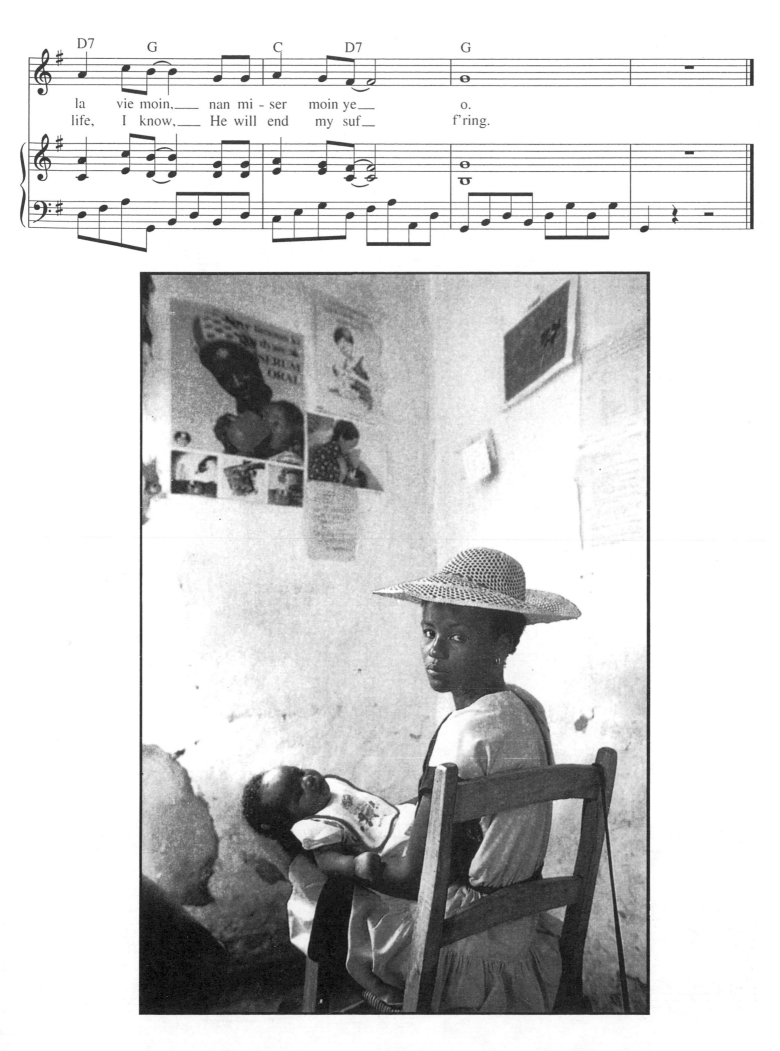

la   vie moin,   nan mi - ser   moin ye   o.
life,   I   know,   He will end   my suf   f'ring.

Flores De Mimé
Flowers Of Mimé

Honduras

A la o - ri - lla del rí - o Ver - be - na de -
On the banks of the rí - o Ver - be - na de -

Ma - ro - mé, Flo - res de mi - mé. Ten -
Ma - ro - mé, Bright mi - mé flow - ers, There

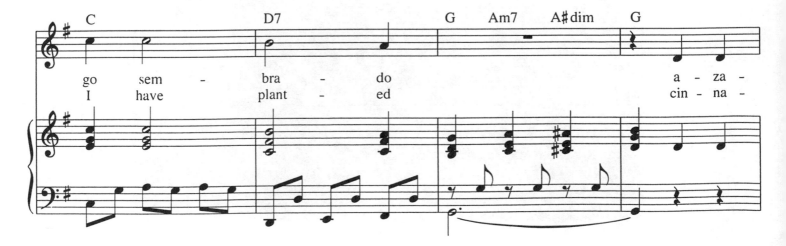

go sem - bra - do a - za -
I have plant - ed cin - na -

En la falda de la montaña
   De Maromé, flores de mimé.
Están sembrando
Un yucal, un cañal y canela
   De Maromé, flores de mimé,
Y maíz morado.

In the foothills of yonder high mountain
In Maromé, bright *mimé* flowers,
They are all planting
Cinnamon, saffron and some verbena,
In Maromé, bright *mimé* flowers,
And purple sweet corn.

Quando quiero cantarle a mi chata
   De Maromé, flores de mimé,
Con mi guitarra,
Ensillo mi caballo plateado,
   De Maromé, flores de mimé,
Y voy montado.

When I want to sing to my sweetheart,
In Maromé, bright *mimé* flowers,
I take my guitar,
Then I saddle my silver-gray pony,
In Maromé, bright *mimé* flowers,
And off I gallop.

Repeat first verse

Papanulan

Honduras

pe - so.   ¡Ay! Pa - pa -
pe - sos.   O! Pa - pa -

nu - lan, Pa - pa - nu - lan, vi - da mí_____ a._____
nu - lan, Pa - pa - nu - lan, my dear sweet___ heart._____

Trabajando el día noche,
Ganancio cuarenta peso,
Ay! Papanulan,
Trabajando el día noche.

Papanulan, Papanulan,
Papanulan, vida mía,
Quiero que si me astumba
Me alegre tamburira.

Night and day you'll find me working,
I earn only forty pesos,
O! Papanulan,
Night and day you'll find me working.

Papanulan, Papanulan,
Papanulan, my dear sweetheart,
I would like that when I'm buried,
You will beat the drum so gaily.

La Llorona
The Weeping Woman

Llorona is often pictured in song as weeping for her dead husband or children. In this love song version, *llorona* is used as a simple refrain.

Mexico

Todos me dicen el negro, llorona, negro pero ___
Ev - 'ry-one calls me the black one, *llo-ro-na*, Yes, black I am, ___

___ ca - ri - ño - so. ___
___ but so lov - ing. ___

Yo soy co - mo el
I'm like the green

___ chi - le ver - de, llo - ro - na, pi - can - te pe - ro sa so
___ chi - le pep - per, *llo-ro-na*, so spic-y but ___ o, so

bro - so._____ Yo ____ ¡Ay de mi! llo -
tast - y._____ I'm ____ Woe is me! llo -

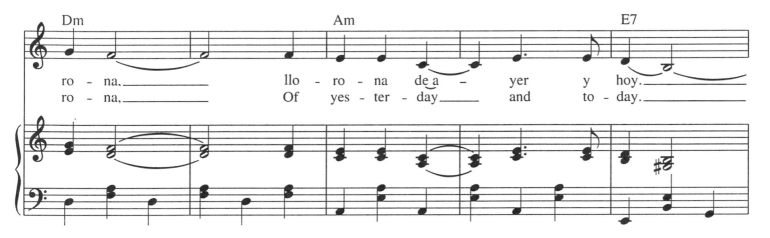

ro - na,_____ llo - ro - na de a - yer y hoy._____
ro - na,_____ Of yes - ter - day____ and to - day._____

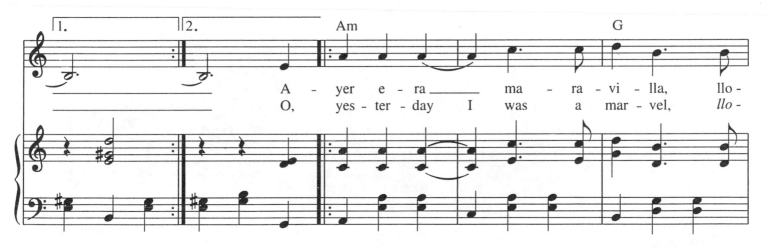

_____ A - yer e - ra____ ma - ra - vi - lla, llo -
_____ O, yes - ter - day I was a mar - vel, *llo -*

ro - na, Y a - ho - ra ni____ som - bra soy._____ A____
ro - na, To - day I am____ just a sha - dow._____ O,

Dicen que no tengo duelo, llorona,)2
porque no me ven llorar.
Hay muertos que no hacen ruido, llorona,)2
y es más grande su penar.

Ay de mí, llorona,
llorona de azul celeste.)2
Y aunque la vida me cueste, llorona,)2
no dejaré de quererte.

Si al cielo subir pudiera, llorona,)2
las estrellas te bajara.
La luna a tus pies pusiera, llorona,)2
con el sol te coronara.

Ay de mí, llorona,
llorona de negros ojos.)2
Ya con ésta se despide, llorona,)2
tu negrito soñador.

People say I'm not in mourning, *llorona*,)2
Because they don't see me crying.
There are deaths that don't make a sound, *llorona*,)2
And whose suffering is so much greater.

Woe is me, *llorona*,
Llorona of heaven's blue color.)2
And even if it costs me my life, *llorona*,)2
I will not cease longing for you.

If I could climb up to the heavens, *llorona*,)2
And bring all the stars down before you,
The moon I would place at your feet, o, *llorona*,)2
And with the bright sun I would crown you.

Woe is me, *llorona*,
Llorona of eyes dark as midnight,)2
And with all this now will be leaving, *llorona*,)2
Your little black heartbroken dreamer.

La Malagueña

The original meaning of *La Malagueña* was a woman from Málaga, Spain. It has become widely recognized as a flamenco dance and virtuoso guitar piece. In this song, the meaning is closer to the original, although the woman in question is now Mexican.

Mexico

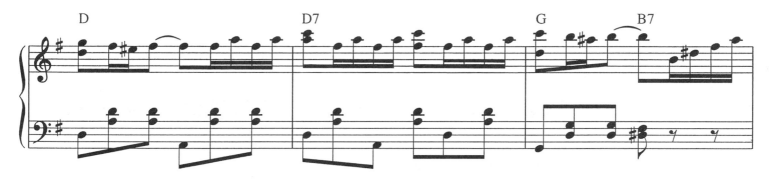

¡Qué bo-
O, your

ni - tos   o - jos   tie - nes_____ de - ba - jo de e- sas dos   ce - jas,_____   de -
eyes they   are so   pret - ty_____ be - neath those two love-ly   eye-brows,_____   be -

ba - jo de e-sas dos ce - jas,_____ qué bo - ni - tos o - jos tie - nes!_____
neath those two love-ly eye-brows,_____ o, your eyes they are so pret - ty!_____

_____ E - llos me quie-ren mi - rar,_____ pe - ro si tú no los
_____ They want to gaze up - on me,_____ but you do not let them

de - jas, _____ pe - ro si tú no los de - jas_____ ni si - quie-ra par - pa -
do it,_____ but you do not let them do it,_____ not e - ven a lit - tle

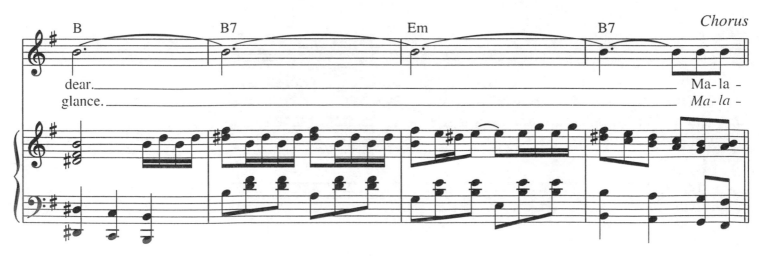

dear._____ Ma-la -
glance._____ Ma-la -

gue - ña sa - le - ro - sa,_____ Be - sar tus la - bios qui - sie - ra,_____
gue - ña, o, so charm-ing,_____ I would kiss your lips with pas-sion,_____

falsetto - yodel

be-sar tus la - bios qui -
yes, kiss your lips with

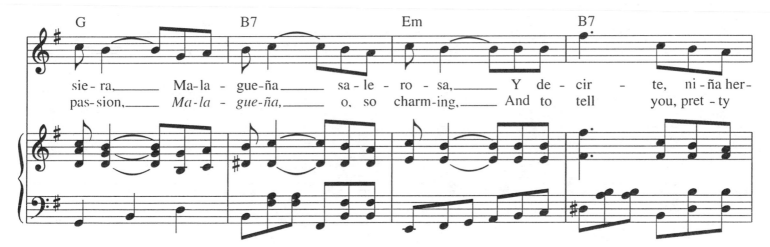

sie - ra,_____ Ma - la - gue - ña_____ sa - le - ro - sa,_____ Y de - cir - te, ni - ña her-
pas-sion,_____ *Ma - la - gue - ña,*_____ o, so charm-ing,_____ And to tell you, pret - ty

mo - sa,_____ e - res lin - da y he-chi - ce - ra, e - res lin - da y he-chi-
la - dy,_____ you are pret - ty and en - chant-ing, you __ are pret-ty and en -

ce - ra,_____ Co - mo el can - dor___ de u - na ro - sa._____ Y de - cir - te ni - ña her

chant - ing,_____ As in - no - cent___ as a rose - bud._____ And to tell you, pret - ty

mo - sa_____ e - res lin - da y he - chi - ce - ra,_____

la - dy,_____ you are pret - ty and en - chant - ing,_____

1.

E - res lin - da y he - chi - ce - ra co - mo el can -

You are pret - ty and en - chant - ing, as in - no -

2.

dor_____ de u - na ro - sa,_____ Si por ce - ra,_____

cent as a rose - bud,_____ If for chant - ing,_____

Co - mo el can - dor   de u - na   ro -   sa.

As in - no - cent   as a   rose -   bud.

Si por pobre me desprecias,
yo te concedo razón,
yo te concedo razón
si por pobre me desprecias.

  Yo no te ofrezco riquezas,
te ofrezco mi corazón,
te ofrezco mi corazón,
a cambio de mi pobreza. *Chorus*

If for poverty you scorn me,
I agree you have good reason,
I agree you have good reason,
If for poverty you scorn me.

  I do not offer you riches,
But I offer you my heart,
But I offer you my heart,
In exchange for my poor fortune. *Chorus*

Hojita De Guarumal
Little Leaf Of The Guarumal

Panama

Ho - ji - ta de gua - ru - mal, Don - de vi - ve la lan - gos - ta, Don - de
Lit-tle leaf of the gua - ru - mal, That's where you can find the lo - cust, And he

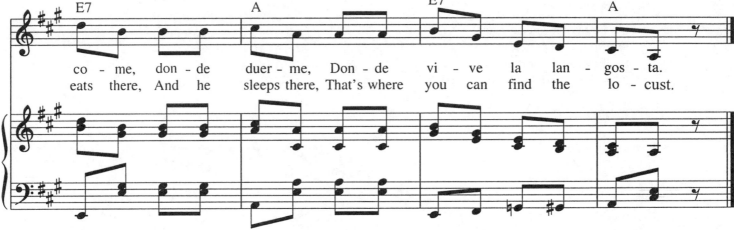

co - me, don - de duer - me, Don - de vi - ve la lan - gos - ta.
eats there, And he sleeps there, That's where you can find the lo - cust.

Hojita de guarumal,
Donde vive la langosta,
Donde come, donde cena,
Donde duerme la langosta.

Hojita de guarumal,
Donde vive la langosta,
Donde come, donde toma,
Donde duerme la langosta.

Hojita de guarumal,
Donde vive la langosta,
Donde come, donde duerme,
Donde muere la langosta.

Little leaf of guarumal,
That's where you can find the locust.
And he eats there, and he sups there,
That's where you can find him sleeping.

Little leaf of the guarumal,
That's where you can find the locust.
And he eats there, and he drinks there,
That's where you can find him sleeping.

Little leaf of guarumal,
That's where you can find the locust.
And he eats there, and he sleeps there,
That's where he will die, the locust.

Mi Pollera
My Skirt

Panama

Mi po - lle - ra, mi po - lle - ra, mi po - lle ra es co - lo - ra - da. Yo quie-ro u-na po-
O, my skirt is, o, My skirt is, O, my skirt's a bright red col - or. I want to have a

lle - ra de o-lán de co-co, Si tú no me las das, Me voy con o - tro. Mi po - ti - go.
skirt made of co - co fi - bre, If you don't give it to me, I will leave you. O, My ev - er

Mi pollera, mi pollera,	O, my skirt is, o, my skirt is,
Mi pollera es colorada.	O, my skirt's a bright red color.
La tuya es blanca, la mía es rosada,	That skirt of yours is snow-white and mine is rosy,
Mi pollera es colorada.	My skirt is a bright red color.
Mi pollera, mi pollera,	O, my skirt is, o, my skirt is,
Mi pollera es colorada.	O, my skirt's a bright red color.
Yo quiero una pollera de olán de hilo.	I really want a skirt with some fancy trimming,
Si tú me la das, me voy contigo.	And if you give it to me, I'm yours forever.

La Guaireñita
The Girl From Guaira

Villarica is the capital of the department of Guaira. A number of words in this song are in the language of the Guaira Indian language: *cuñata-î* means girl; the second line of verse two is translated in the English version; *yboty* means flowers.

Paraguay

Es Vi - lla - ri - ca u — na vi - lla her - mo - sa,___
Yes Vi - lla - ri - ca's___ a might - y fine___ town,

De don - de sur - je___ cu - ña - ta - î.___
My sweet - heart's from there,___ Now, don't you see.___

Lle - na de flo - res___ en sus jar - di - nes,___
Cov - ered with flow - ers,___ gar - dens full of them,___

Vi - va la pa - tria_____ del__ Y - bo - ty!_____
Long live the home-land_____ of__ Y - bo - ty!_____

D

Allí yo tengo mi prometida,
Yporanüégpe na mboyoyai,
Como el lucero de la mañana
Que anuncia el bello co'embotá.

That's where she does live, my promised sweetheart,
The prettiest girl I ever did see;
Just like the bright star that dawns in the morning,
And that announces a pleasant day.

Noches Paraguayas
Paraguayan Evenings

Paraguay

By Martita Ramirez

No-ches pa-ra-gua-yas,_____ ba-jo tus es-tre-llas,_
Pa-ra-gua-yan eve-nings,_____ un-der-neath your star-light,_

Me ha-go mil pre-gun-tas_____ en mi so-le-dad;_____
Ask a thous-and ques-tions,_____ In my sol-i-tude;_____

Can-to es-ta güa-ran-ia,_____ en mis ti-bias no-ches,_
I sing this *güa-ran-ia*,_____ in my sum-mer eve-nings,_

a mi a-mor au - sen-te,_____ que le - jos es - tá.
to my ab- sent lov- er,_____ who is far a - way.

que le - jos es - tá._____
who is far a - way._____

Noches Paraguayas,   Paraguayan evenings,
Beso así tu suelo.   Thus I kiss your soil,
Soñando nostalgias   Bittersweetly dreaming
En mi Paraguay.   In my Paraguay.
    Canto esta güarania   I sing this *güarania*,
    En mis tibias noches,   In my summer evenings,
    A mi amor ausente,   To my absent lover,
    Que lejos está.   Who is far away.

Repeat first verse

Llanto Del Indio
Lament Of The Indian

Atahualpa was the last Inca ruler. He was defeated by the Spaniards in 1532. Sigalpa was one of his brave generals.

Peru

Yaraví

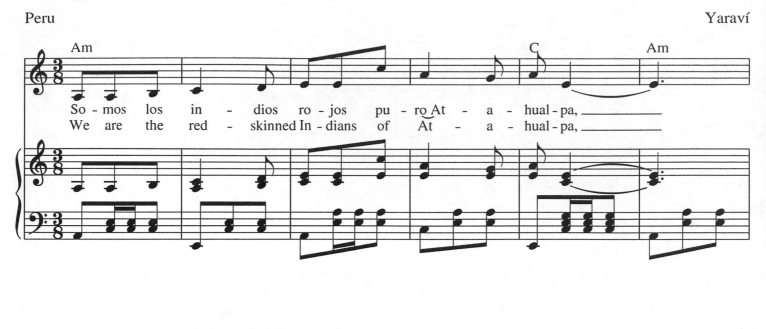

So - mos los in - dios ro - jos pu - ro At - a - hual - pa,_____
We are the red - skinned In - dians of At - a - hual - pa,_____

Que en nues - tra a - tri - ción so - mos co - mo Si - gal - pa._____
And in our sad - ness we are just like Si - gal - pa._____

Cuan-do la lu - na sa - le des - te
And when the moon ap - pears in the

de_el o - rien - te,_____ A - lum - bran nues - tras
east - ern heav - ens,_____ Our souls and our minds

al - mas y nues - tras men - tes._____
light up with hope e - ter - nal._____

Somos los indios rojos puro Atahualpa,
que en nuestra atrición somos como Sigalpa.
Todos dicen que el indio llora en sus quenas,
porque canta con alma sus crueles penas.

We are the red-skinned Indians of Atahualpa,
And in our sadness we are just like Sigalpa.
Everyone says the Indian's music's crying;
He sings his heartfelt songs - he can't stop his sighing.

Muchacha Bonita
Pretty Girl

Peru

Huayno

Mu - cha - cha bo - ni - ta lu - nar en la ca - ra
The beau - ty spot on your face makes you look pret - ty,

si e - res sol - te - ra da - me tu a - mor, Mu -
If you're not mar - ried, give me your love, O

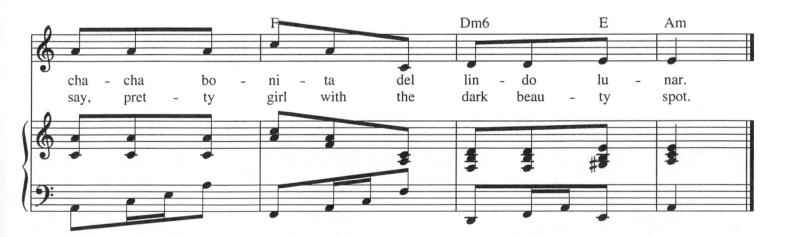

cha - cha bo - ni - ta del lin - do lu - nar.
say, pret - ty girl with the dark beau - ty spot.

Mas si has dado a alguno tu vida y tu amor,
Vete bien lejos, lejos de mí,
Muchacha bonita del lindo lunar.

But if you have given your life and your love,
Go far away - so far off from me,
You dear pretty girl with the dark beauty spot.

Problema Social
Social Problem

This song was written by a Puerto Rican in New York in the mid-1940s.

Puerto Rico

By Eduardo Reyes

De un — a_is - li - ta del Ca - ri - be
From   a   Car - ib - be - an   is - land,

En bus - ca de tra - ba - jo ven - go yo.   A -
Look - ing for a job I ar - rived in town.   But

som - bra - do me que - dé   con lo que en - con - tré   A -
what was my big sur - prise!   I can't be - lieve my eyes!   Sur -

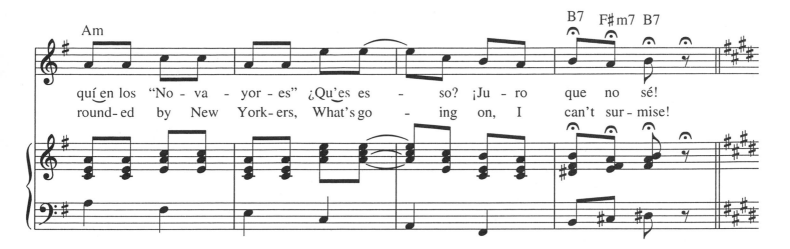

qui en los "No - va - yor - es" ¿Qu'es es - so? ¡Ju - ro que no sé!
round- ed by New York- ers, What's go - ing on, I can't sur - mise!

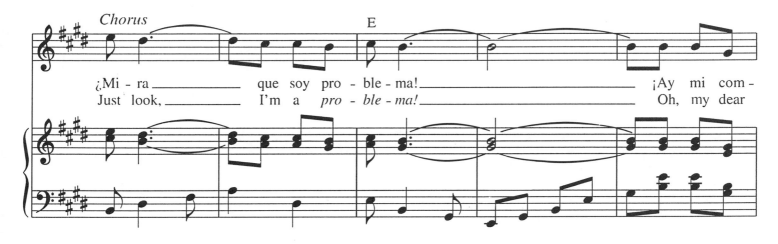

Chorus

¿Mi - ra que soy pro - ble - ma! ¡Ay mi com -
Just look, I'm a *pro - ble - ma!* Oh, my dear

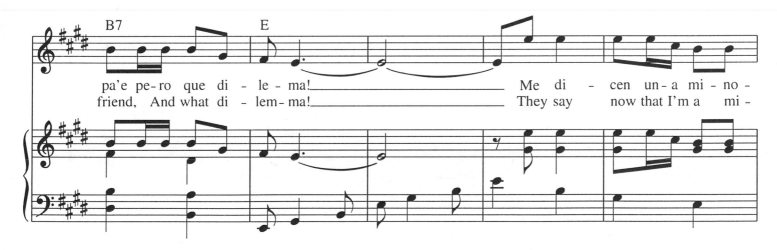

pa'e pe- ro que di - le - ma! Me di - cen un- a mi - no -
friend, And what di - lem- ma! They say now that I'm a mi -

rí - a; Pro - ble - ma en so- cio- lo - gí - a.
nor- i- ty; A big pro - blem in so- ci - ol- o- gy.

Quie - ro _____ so - lo ga - nar un - os _____ bo - los _____ pa' la de -
I want _____ to earn some mon - ey here _____ so that _____ I can sup -

fen - sa _____ del hu - mil - de ho - gar. Yo no ven - go a pe -
port my _____ hum - ble fam - i - ly. I don't come ask - ing _

- dir li - mos - na. Lo que quier - o es só - lo tra - ba - jar.
_ cha - ri - ty. _ What I want now is job se - cu - ri - ty.

Yo, que peleaba en la guerra,	I, who soldiered in the army,
Americano al fín, como nací.	An American, as good as anyone.
Aunque sirvo pa' pelear,	The gun I had to tote
Yo no puedo votar	Did not get me the vote
Pa' el presidente de la patria,	For President, and when I look
Y al venir a trabajar. *Chorus*	For a job, I get their goat. *Chorus*

Un Jíbaro En Nueva York
A Peasant In New York

Puerto Rico

This ten-line verse is called a *décima* A typical *décima* is frequently improvised by the singer, who may be challenged to create clever, humorous rhymes on the spot.

Me di - jis-te hay co-mo un mes que tu hab-las cual - quier id -
A month a - go you did say, Each and ev -'ry lan - guage you're

io - ma y a - ho - ra yo no ha - go bro-ma y tien-es que hab-lar in - glés
know-ing, Now's the time that you must be show-ing, So speak in En-glish to - day

Ar - ro - dí - lla - te a mis pies sin a - lar-des y sin
Now, kneel down here at my feet, And don't make an - y ex -

76

ruí - dos, ___   Y di - me en ver - so me - di - do, ___
cu - ses, ___   But tell me in meas-ured ver - ses, ___

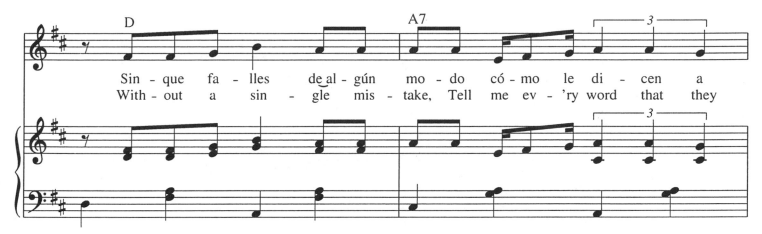

Sin - que fa - lles de al - gún mo - do có - mo le di - cen a
With - out a sin - gle mis - take, Tell me ev - 'ry word that they

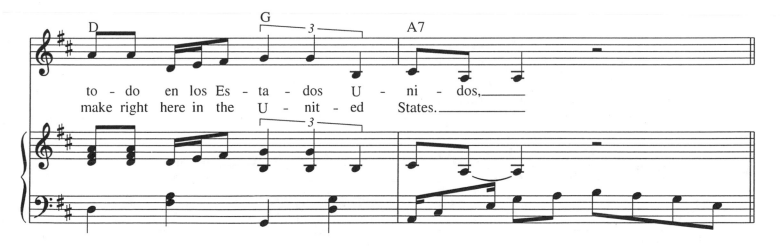

to - do en los Es - ta - dos U - ni - dos, ___
make right here in the U - nit - ed States. _____

Man

A la puer - ta, di - cen "door." ___   Al se - ñor, le di - cen,
For *la puer-ta,* They say "door." ___   For *se - ñor,* They call him

Woman

Hay alguna analogía
En lo que me has contestado,
Pero aún no has terminado,
Falta mucho todavía.
La vida me apostaría,
Que aunque tomes interés,
Si te diera todo el mes
El chance para pensar,
Tú no podrás hilvanar
Otra décima en inglés.

Man

Al beso le dicen "kiss,"
Para decir la hora le dicen "o'clock,"
Y a la señorita, "miss."
Al queso le dicen "cheese,"
Al te amo, "I love you,"
Al orgullo, "ballyhoo."
Le dicen "house" a la casa,
Y para decir "¿Qué pasa?"
"What's the matter with you?"

Woman

Aunque de todas las redes
Saliste don facultad,
Tengo la seguridad,
Que finalizar no quedes.
Lo van a escuchar ustedes,
Qué por su derrota brindo.
Porque sólo cuando eres gringo,
Como aquel guerrero fuerte,
Que dijo al pie de la muerte,
"Muero, pero no me rindo."

Man

Y dicen al día, "day,"
Al pobre le dicen "poor."
Al tan bello, "so beautiful,"
Y a lo que está bien, "okay."
Y como cosa de ley,
A la luna dicen "moon."
Al tono le dicen "tune,"
Y en vez de fín dicen "end."
Venga un aplauso, *my friend,*
Que venga, *very soon.*

Woman

There are some words you do know.
But though you think you are winning,
This is just the very beginning,
You've still a long way to go.
I'd bet my life on it now,
That even if you would wish
To spend another month there,
To rack your brains for a rhyme,
You couldn't make up in time
Another *décima* in English.

Man

They call *beso* "kiss,"
To tell time they say "o'clock,"
And *señorita* they call "miss."
Queso becomes "cheese,"
For *te amo* they say "I love you,"
Orgullo is "ballyhoo."
They say "house" for *casa,*
And for *"¿Qué pasa?"* they say,
"What's the matter with you?"

Woman

Though you have made no mistakes,
With all the traps I have set you,
I am willing to bet you,
You don't have what it takes,
I celebrate your defeat.
For you will only speak the lingo
When you have become a *gringo.*
Like that warrior of old,
Who, when facing death, I'm told,
Said "I die, but don't surrender."

Man

They call *día* "day,"
For *pobre,* they say "poor."
Tan bello is "so beautiful,"
And what's *bien* is "okay."
And, as the law goes,
Luna is called "moon."
A *tono* is a "tune,"
Instead of *fin* they'll say "end."
Let's hear some applause, my friend,
Let's hear it very soon.

79

La Terrible Inmensidad
The Terrible Immensity

Uruguay

La te-rri-ble in-men-si-dad _____ en mi des-car-ga sus-pi - ra.
How this im-men - si - ty weighs down, Caus-ing me ev - er to sigh,_____

Los pla-ce-res son men-ti - ra;
Pleas-ures are noth- ing but false-hoods,

Só-lo la pe-na es ver-dad._____
On-ly hard-ship is the truth,_____

Chorus

E - sa tu sed de
While for life you are

vi - da,_____ Me tie - ne siem-pre pe - nan - do._____
thirst-ing,_____ It on - ly height-ens the sor - row._____

Con mi destino luchando,
Y sin encontrar bonanza,
Sufriendo está mi esperanza,
Dime, fortuna, ¿hasta cuándo? *Chorus*

I with my destiny fighting,
Never encountering fortune.
Suffering is all I can hope for.
Tell me, o fortune: for how long? *Chorus*

Sentimientos
Feelings

Uruguay   Milonga

The *milonga* is a type of folk ballad, known in Uruguay since the middle of the 19th century. Sung by *milongueros*, it may deal with a variety of subjects, from politics and nationalism to "*la conquista de una mujer*" ("the conquest of a woman"). "Sentimientos" is in the ten-line, *décima*, form. The manner of expression in this song is rather convoluted. The repeated first words of each verse — a sort of litany — actually interrupt the flow of thought. The sentence fragments should be judiciously pieced together to make sense out of the tortured soul of the singer. As with its equivalent, the Argentine tango, a *milonga* is invariably a song of sadness and suffering.

Di - go   que sien - to des - ve - lo,   Di - go   que sien - to a-flic - ción,
I   say   that I'm   feel-ing rest - less   I   say   that I'm feel-ing grief,

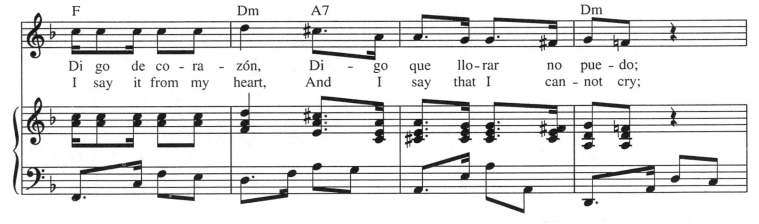

Di - go   de co - ra - zón,   Di - go   que llo-rar   no pue - do;
I   say   it from my heart,   And   I   say   that I   can - not cry;

Di - go   que en mi tris-te sue - lo,   Di - go   que pa - dez-co, sí,
I   say   that in my sad coun-try,   I   say   I do suf-fer so,

82

Salvo estoy de mi entender,	I am beyond understanding,
Salvo de hacer exigencias,	I am beyond all demands.
Salvo de correspondencia,	I am beyond doing favors,
Salvo me tiene un deber;	I'm beyond all things like that.
Salvo de todo placer,	I am beyond any pleasure,
Salvo estoy porque comprendo,	I am beyond, for I know,
Salvo de una dicha vengo,	I'm beyond, I come from fortune.
Salvo de un buen porvenir,	I am beyond a good future.
Salvo vivo de morir,	I am beyond even dying;
DE UN SENTIMIENTO QUE TENGO.	FROM A FEELING THAT I HAVE.
Quisiera que el más cantor,	I'd like that the finest singer,
Quisiera un consejo darme,	I'd like to get his advice.
Quisiera nunca acordarme,	I'd like never to remember,
Quisiera tener valor;	I'd like never having courage.
Quisiera en este dolor,	I'd like to in all of this pain,
Quisiera hacer dividir,	I'd like to divide it up.
Quisiera para vivir,	I'd like in order to live,
Quisiera el alma serena,	I'd like my soul to be peaceful.
Quisiera apartar las penas,	I'd like to put aside suffering,
QUE HE SENTIDO SIN SENTIR.	THAT I HAVE FELT WITHOUT FEELING.
Tengo en el sentido valor,	I have a feeling of courage,
Tengo cambiado el pesar,	I have changed all of my sorrow.
Tengo que recuperar,	I have to find once again,
Tengo la esperanza en Dios;	I have my faith in the Lord God.
Tengo en este gran dolor,	I have in this mighty aching,
Tengo el alma batiendo,	I have my soul in torment.
Tengo que vivir sufriendo,	I have to live in suffering,
Tengo una pequeña duda,	I have a small doubting question,
Tengo en mi mente segura,	I have in my mind for sure,
QUE ESTOY SIN SENTIR SINTIENDO.	THAT I AM FEELING NO FEELING.

La Mónica Pérez
Monica Perez

A *joropo* is a lively dance.

Venezuela   Joropo

Señora Mó-ni-ca Pé-rez, a mi me pa-re-ce bien,
Señora Mó-ni-ca Pé-rez, it sure does ap-pear to me,

Que em-pa-te-mos los a-mo-res, Si es que lo con-sien-te us-té.
That we should cut short our love, If that is what you real-ly want.

Se-ño-ra Mó-ni-ca Pé-rez, Mi pa-dri-no me en-se-
Se-ño-ra Mó-ni-ca Pé-rez, My grand-fa-ther, he taught

ñó   a to-mar lo que qui-sie-ra y a us-
me   to take what I want and as for me, I

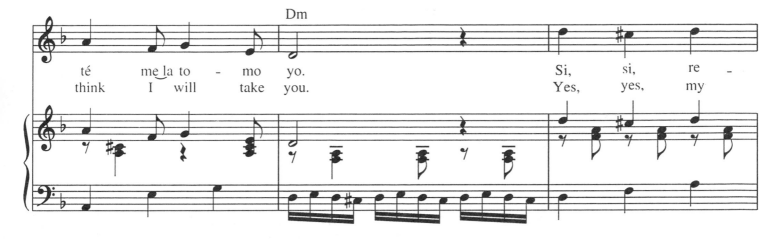

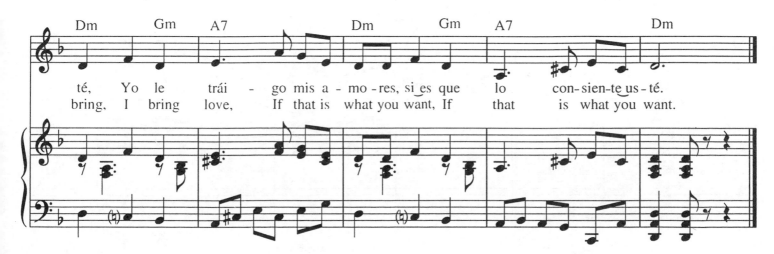

El Carite
The Kingfish

Venezuela

A - yer sa - lió la lan - cha *Nue-va Es - par - ta.* Sa - lió con -
The *Nue-va Es - par - ta* set sail yes - ter - day.___ Set out so

fia - da a re - co - rrer los ma - res. En - con - tró un pez de
brave - ly to sail a - cross the o - cean. It met a fish that

fuer - zas muy li - je - ro, Que a - ga - rra los an - zue - los y re - vien - ta los gua -
was so ver - y trick - y, It grap - pled with our fish hooks and it smashed up our fish

Chorus

ra - les, Co - mo la cos-ta es bo - ni - ta, Yo me ven - go di - vir -
box - es. O, The coast-line is so pret - ty, As I sailed___ a - long for

tien - do;   Pe - ro____ me vie - ne si - guien - do de fue - ra u - na pi - ra - gui - ta.
pleas - ure;   But I____ saw ap - proach - ing swift - ly a ca - noe off in the dis - tance.

Ayer salimos muy temprano a pescar
Nos fuimos juntos todos los pescadores
Y entre las olas lo vimos saltando
Que iba persiguiendo a los voladores. *Chorus*

We sailed out early yesterday to fish,
And we were joined by all the fishermen.
Among the waves we saw how it did leap,
As it did chase the silver flying fish. *Chorus*

Un marinero al verlo se alegró
A este sabroso pescado de los mares
Y en seguida les dijo a los muchachos
Preparen los arpones y tiren los guarales. *Chorus*

And when a sailor spied him, he was glad
To see this tasty fish of the deep ocean.
So he then called out loudly to his shipmates,
"Prepare the harpoons, heave away so lively!" *Chorus*

En los ramales del coco lo pescamos
En lo profundo del mar donde vivía
Y lo pescamos en la lancha *Nueva Esparta*.
Para presentarlo hoy con alegría. *Chorus*

With our long lines of fiber we did fish it,
Down to the depths where he lived in the ocean.
And we did catch him in the launch *Nueva Esparta*,
To show it off today with great emotion. *Chorus*

Señores, todos les damos las gracias
Los pescadores se van a marchar.
Nos despedimos con este carite
Que les presentamos en este lugar. *Chorus*

Good people, we so gratefully do thank you
And now the fishermen are ready to move on.
We take our leave with our great *carite*,
Which we have shown you here in our town. *Chorus*